THE GUDE AND GODLIE BALLATIS

THE GUDE AND GODLIE BALLATIS

EDITED BY

IAIN ROSS

PUBLISHED FOR

THE SALTIRE SOCIETY

BY

OLIVER AND BOYD LTD

FIRST PUBLISHED 1940
REPRINTED 1957

PRINTED IN GREAT BRITAIN
BY BRADFORD AND DICKENS
DRAYTON HOUSE, LONDON W.C.1

PREFACE

THE earliest known edition of the *Gude and Godlie Ballatis* belongs to the year 1567. There is strong reason to suppose earlier editions, perhaps about 1540 or 1546, and even before then many of the poems in the book may have been circulated as broadsheets. Several of them are translations from German hymns of Luther and his followers. Traces are also found of Swiss, French, and Swedish influence. The whole collection is markedly Lutheran in its ideas.

It falls into four sections. The first consists of a catechism of doctrine, written in prose, and then in verse. This is followed by sixteen " Spirituall Sangis " of a very didactic and sometimes verbose nature. Then come " Certaine Ballatis of the Scripture," twenty in all, beginning with the fine poem :

"Till Christ quhome I am haldin for to lufe,"

after which come " The Psalmes of David, with uther new Pleasand Ballatis." This last section has in the earliest edition 63 poems, and 68 in the other editions extant. In nature they vary greatly, from devotional poetry and paraphrase of considerable merit to scurrilous satires and somewhat clumsy religious adaptations of popular songs, such as " Johne, cum kis me now." Such adaptations were no new thing, being known certainly in England and Germany during Catholic times.

During the formative period of the religious revolution in Scotland, before the firm establishment of

Calvinism in the seventeenth century, editions of the ballads seem to have been numerous. Their Lutheran doctrine probably accounts for the obscurity which covers them so completely, after 1630-40, that to-day we can trace only four early editions, those of 1567, 1578, 1600 and 1621 : and altogether only five complete extant copies of the book.

The authorship of *The Gude and Godlie Ballatis* is still a possible subject of controversy. It is almost certain, however, that the main responsibility for the book rests with one John Wedderburn of Dundee, helped, it is thought, by his brothers James and Robert. John Wedderburn was a contemporary of Patrick Hamilton at the University of St Andrews, about 1525 to 1528, in which year he took the Master's degree. According to one theory he was then priest for some short time in Dundee, until in 1539 or 1540 he fled to Wittemberg, where he spent several years, and where his brothers may have joined him. With the Protestant triumph he was able to return to Scotland somewhere about 1546. Of the later years of his life nothing is certain, although there are grounds for supposing that he, or his brother Robert, may have been still alive when the *Ballatis* were reprinted in 1578, with several additions.

Modern editions are few. The text of 1578 was reprinted by Dr Laing in 1868, and in 1897 the Scottish Text Society published the text of 1567, edited, with very valuable notes, by Dr A. F. Mitchell, at one time Professor of Ecclesiastical History in St Andrews. To both these this selection owes much.

The main effort in compiling the selection has been to represent as exactly as possible the varied nature of the complete work. Consequently much of considerable merit has been omitted, which personal bias would have wished to include, *e.g.* the burial hymn, which begins

> " Our brother let us put in grave."

The text is based on that of 1578 mainly, and evidence of the uncertain spelling which was common then has been allowed to stand. Notes have been cut to a minimum. For fuller details on matters of origin, text, or accompanying music readers may turn to Dr Mitchell's edition, which is available in most big libraries. It has, of course, a strong Presbyterian bias in some of its comments. That, however, does not concern us here, where the work undertaken is provision of a text on which discussion may be based.

In conclusion, it may be permissible to express the hope that this edition will contradict two common impressions : first, the opinion that *The Gude and Godlie Ballatis* were mainly satirical rhymes and poor religious parodies of popular songs ; and secondly, the simplification which sees in the history of sixteenth century Scotland a national adoption of Calvinism as something specially adapted to what is vaguely called " the Scottish character." Perhaps, of course, these opinions are already dead.

I. R.

September 1939.

NOTE

-and = *-ing*, e.g. " ringand," " prayand."
qu   = *w*, e.g. " quhat," " quhome."
oi   = *ō*, e.g. " moir," " gloir," " loist."
y   = *i*, e.g. " lyfe," " stryfe."
-ocht = *-ought*, e.g. " bocht," " thocht."[1]
-is, plural ending, fully pronounced in two-syllable words, *e.g.*
     " The hillis dansit, and lichtly lap lyke lambis," but given
     the value of *s* in longer words, *e.g.* " tabillis," " adderis."
-aif = *-ave.*
y (consonant) = *g* before a vowel, *e.g.* " foryet," " unfeinyeitlie."

[1] " thocht " is often " although," as on pp. 13, 16, 29, 48, 62.

A

I

Moyses upon the mount Sinay,
with the greit God spak face for face,
Fastand and prayand but delay,
The tyme of fourtie dayis space.
    O God be mercyfull to us.

And God gave him thir [1] ten commandis,
To teiche to mankinde everie ane,
And wrait them with his awin handis
Twyse on twa tabillis maid of stane.
    O God be mercyfull to us.

i. I am thy God allanerlie,[2]
    Serve me in feir and faith thairfoir,
    Wirschip na kinde of Imagerie,
    And give na creature my gloir.
        O God be mercyfull to us.

ij. Tak nocht the Name of God in vaine,
    Bot let your talk be nay and ye,
    Except ane Judge do yow constraine
    To testifie the veritie.
        O God be mercyfull to us.

iij. Wirk na evill wark on Haly day,
    Fle from all sinfull lust and sleuth,[3]
    Walk and be sober, fast and pray,
    Heir him that preiche the word of treuth.
        O God be mercyfull to us.

---

[1] these   [2] only   [3] sloth

iiij. Honour thy Elders, and them supplie,
Geve that thair neid of the requyre,
Obey all Judges in thair degre,
Ordand [1] ouir the to have impyre.
O God be mercyfull to us.

v. Thow sall not slay in na kin wyse,[2]
In counsell, thocht, nor outward deid.
Be thow ane Judge, or on ane Syse,[3]
In judgement ordourly proceid.
O God be mercyfull to us.

vj. Commit na kinde of licherie,
Bot leve ane chaist and sober lyfe :
Want thow the gift of Chaistitie
Burne not in lust, bot wed ane wyfe.
O God be mercyfull to us.

vij. Commit na thift, na man thow reif,[4]
Leve on thy wage, thy rent or wark :
Hald na mannis geir,[5] let nane the craif,[6]
Beg not and thow be haill and stark.[7]
O God be mercyfull to us.

viij. Beir na witnes with fals report,
In contrair just and richteous men :
Defame na man in ony sort,
Suppois his fault or vice thow ken.
O God be mercyfull to us.

ix. Thy Nichtbouris wyfe, hous, heritage,
Thow covet not to the, nor wis
His hors, his oxe, his maid, nor page,
Nor ony gudis that is his.
O God be mercyfull to us.

[1] ordained   [2] kind of way   [3] Assize   [4] rob
[5] property   [6] importune   [7] sound and strong

x. Our poysound nature (allace thairfoir)
Can never mair this Law fulfill,
Bot grevand God ay moir and moir,
And can not wirk his godly will.
    O God be mercyfull to us.

Then quhy gave God to us this Law ?
The quhilk [1] be na way we can keip ?
That we be it our Sin suld knaw,
Repent and mend, and for it weip.
    O God be mercyfull to us.

Trew faith in Christ wirkand [2] be lufe,
Sall save us from the fyre of hell :
Thocht Goddis Angell wald this reprufe,[3]
As fals and cursit ye him expell.
    O God be mercyfull to us.

2

We trow [4] in God allanerlie,
Full of all micht and Maiestie,
Maker of hevin and eird [5] sa braid,
Quhilk [1] hes him self our Father maid :
And we his sonnis ar in deid,
He will us keip in all our neid,
Baith saull and body to defend,
That na mischance sall us offend ;
He takis cure [6] baith day and nicht,
To save us throw his godly micht
Fra Sathanis subteltie [7] and slicht.

---

[1] who, which   [2] working   [3] reprove   [4] believe
      [5] earth   [6] care   [7] cunning

We trow in Jesus Christ his Sone,
God, lyke in gloir, our Lord alone ;
Quhilk, for his mercy and his grace,
Wald man be borne to mak our peace,
Of Mary mother Virgin chaist
Consavit be the Haly Gaist.
And for our saik on croce did die,
Fra sin and hell to mak us fre :
And rais from deith, throw his Godheid,
Our Mediatour and our remeid,[1]
Sall cum to Judge baith quick and deid.

We trow in God the Haly Spreit,
In all distres our comfort sweit.
We trow the Kirk Catholick be,
And faithfull Christin companie,
Throw all the warld with ane accord.
Remissioun of our sin we trow ;
And this same flesche that levis now
Sall stand up at the latter day,
And bruik [2] Eternall lyfe for ay.

3

Christ baptist was be Johne in Jordan flude,[3]
  For to fulfil for us all richteousnes,
And our Baptisme dotit [4] with sanctitude,
  And greit vertew, to wesche [5] our sinfulnes,
  To drowne the deid,[6] and hell for to oppres,
Quhen Goddis word with water joynit be,
Throw faith to gif [7] us life Eternallie.

---

[1] remedy   [2] enjoy, possess   [3] flood   [4] endowed
[5] wash   [6] death   [7] give

For our waiknes, God of his mercy sweit
   To strenth our Faith ordand this Sacrament,
In name of Father, Sone and Haly Spreit,
   To wesche our body, and in our minde to prent [1]
   That word and water outward represent,
Throw wirking of the Spirit into our hart,
That Christis blude weschis away the sin inwart. [2]

Our Baptisme is ane takin, [3] and ane signe,
   That auld Adame suld drownit be and die,
And gravit in the deid [4] of Christ our King,
   To rise with him to life Eternallie :
   That is, we suld our sin ay mortifie,
Resistand vice, leif haly, just and trew,
And throw the Spirit daylie our life renew.

Be figure and be word, Christ did us teiche,
   The Fatheris voyce was hard [5] sayand full cleir,
Jesus, quhome I have send my word to preiche,
   He is my wellbelovit Sone sa deir,
   In word, in wark, allone ye sall him heir :
In him is all my plesour and delyte,
To him I yow commit baith small and greit.

The Haly Gaist come [6] downe to testifie,
   His doctrine and his Baptisme to declair,
In form of Dow [7] sat on him soberlie [8] :
   In Baptisme to dout not nor dispair,
   Baith Father, Sone, and Haly Gaist ar thair
To be our gyde, [9] the Trinitie him sell [10]
Hes gevin, in eird with us to dwell.

---

[1] imprint   [2] inward   [3] token
[4] buried in the death   [5] heard   [6] came
[7] dove   [8] quietly   [9] guide   [10] self

Christ bad his Apostillis preiche to all creature
    That thay with sin and hell war all forlorne ;
Quha will beleve, and traist my wordis sure
    And baptist is, and new againe is borne,
    And Sathan and all his warkis hes forsworne,
Thay sall be saif, and never mair sall die,
Bot ring [1] in gloir perpetuall with me.

Quha will not this greit grace beleve, to hell
    Salbe [2] condempnit, with eternall deid [3]
Quhair Purgatorie and Pardounis will not sell,
    And gude intent, thair Pylate plicht [4] and leid [5] :
    Dum ceremonies, the quhilk themself hes maid
And wowis [6] vaine, quhilk thay did never keip,
Sall gar thame gnashe thair teith, and eyis weip.

Our eine [7] seis outward bot the water cauld,
    Bot our pure faith the power spirituall
Of Christis blude, inwart it dois behauld,
    Quhilk is ane levand [8] well celestiall
    Yit for to purge the penitent with all,
Our native sin in Adame to expell,
And all trespas committit be oursell.

Our Baptisme is not done all on ane day,
    Bot all our lyfe it lestis identlie [9] :
Remissioun of our sin induris for ay :
    For thocht [10] we fall, throw grit fragylitie,
    The cunnand,[11] anis contract faithfullie
Be our grit God at Font, sall ever remaine,
Als oft as we repent, and sin refraine.

---

[1] reign   [2] shall be   [3] death   [4] plea
[5] cry   [6] vows   [7] eyes   [8] living
     [9] steadily   [10] although   [11] covenant

We can not give to God loving conding [1]
  For sa greit grace, and mercy infinite,
Quhilk institute this Sacrament and Sing,[2]
  Quhais greit vertew in veirs I can not dyte [3] ;
  Bot mony cunning Clerk of it dois wryte
Full Christianely, als the Catechisme buke
Declaris at lenth, quha list [4] to luke.

4

  Our Saviour Christ, King of grace,
  With God the Father maid our peace ;
  And with his bludie woundis fell,[5]
  Hes us redemit from the Hell.

  And he, that we suld not foryet,
  Gave us his body for to eit
  In forme of breid, and gave us syne [6]
  His blude to drink in forme of wyne.

  Quha will ressave this Sacrament,
  Suld have trew faith, and sin repent ;
  Quha usis it unworthelie,
  Ressavis deid [7] eternallie.

  We suld [8] to God give praise and gloir,
  That sched his blude us to restoir ;
  Eit this in his remembrance,
  In signe of thy delyverance.

  Thow suld not dout, bot fast beleve,
  That Christis body sall releve
  All them that ar in hevines
  Repentand sair thair sinfulnes.

[1] fitting   [2] Sign   [3] write   [4] chooses
[5] keen   [6] after   [7] death   [8] should

Sic grace and mercy nane can craif
Bot thay that troublit hartis haif :
Feill [1] thow then sin, abstene thy sell,
Or thy rewaird sall be in hell.

Christ sayis, Sinners cum unto me,
Quhilk myster [2] hes of my mercie :
Neidis thow nocht my medicine,
I lose my paine and travel tyne.[3]

Gif thow thy self thy Saull culd win,
In vaine I deit for thy sin :
My Supper is nocht graithit [4] for the,
Gif thow can mak thy self supplie.

Will thow thy sinfull life confes,
And with this wark thy faith expres,
Sa ar ye worthie, small and greit,
And it sall strenth your faith perfite.

And thow sall thankfull be thairfoir,
And love thy God for evermoir ;
Thy Nichtbour lufe, and als supplie
His neid, as Christ hes done for the.

---

[1] understand   [2] need   [3] labour loose   [4] made ready

Certaine Spirituall Sangis, togidder with ane
Confessioun of Sin, and ane Prayer

5

Sore I complaine of Sin,
   And with King David weip ;
I feill my hart within
   The wraith of God full deip.
I wyte [1] my greit trespas
   Is caus of all my wo,
Quhairwith God grevit was
   Full sore, and oft also.

O God ! I me confes
   Ane sinfull creature,
Full of all wretchitnes
   Fragill, vaine, vyle and pure.
Thair is na gude in me
   Bot pryde, lust, and desyre,
And warldis vanitie,
   The way to hellis fyre.

Except God do me save
   From hell and endles paine,
My sin will me dissave,
   Quhilk I can not refraine.
My only hope and traist,
   Help my fragillitie
My sinnis to detest,
   Resistand constantlie.

O cast me not away
   For my greit sinne, O Lord,
I grant my vices all
   Blasphemit hes thy word.

[1] know

God, for thy greit mercie,
    And Christis woundis wyde,
Ane steidfast faith grant me
    Allone to be my gyde.

Christ, Goddis Sone allone,
    Victour of deid and hell,
Thow tuke my nature one
    My sinnis to expell,
And gaif thyself to plaige,[1]
    Me cative [2] to convoy,
To my richt heritage,
    From paine to hevinlie joy.

Thy servand Lord defend,
    Quhome thow hes bocht sa deir ;
Trew preichours [3] to me send
    Thy word to schaw me cleir :
Lat me my lyfe amend,
    And thairin perseveir,
Grant me ane blyssit end
    Quhen I sall part from heir.

O Lord God, Haly Spreit,
    Full of benignitie,
Trew Christis promeis sweit,
    Teiche me the veritie.
Expell my ignorance,
    My sinnis mortifie,
Grant me perseverance,
    Unto the end trewlie.

---

[1] pledge   [2] wretched   [3] preachers

6

Faithfull in Christ, use your riches richt,
　　Not to your lust and sensualitie :
Bot all tyme help the pure with all your micht,
　　For in the frute sall knawin be the tre ;
　　And gude and evill sall baith rewardit be,
With hevinlie gloir, and hell sa terrabill,
To that effect spak Christ this parabill :—

Ane certaine man was riche, and coistly cled
　　With purpour [1] sylk, heich [2] and presumpteous,
And everie day deliciously him fed :
　　Thair was alswa [3] a pure hecht [4] Lazarus,
　　Lay seik at the yet [5] of this gluttounis hous ;
Throw sairis [6] smart he had ane peirles pyne,[7]
And wantit fude, quhen he wald [8] fainest dyne.

To satisfie his seikly [9] appetyte,
　　He wald have eitin of the crummis small,
Quhilk fell downe fra his burde [10] of greit delyte ;
　　But nane to gif [11] him was sa liberall :
　　The doggis did thair office naturall,
And oft thay did this catyve [12] man refresche,
Lickand the filth furth [13] of his laithly [14] flesche.

It chancit sa this begger did deceis,
　　Syne caryit [15] was be angels gracious
In Abrahams bosome, in hevinly rest and peace.
　　And this riche man that was sa ryatous,[16]
　　Deceissit als,[17] syne buryit glorious ;
In hellis paine he lyftit up his eine,[18]
And syne afar of Abraham hes he sene.

[1] purple	[2] high	[3] also	[4] called	[5] gate
[6] sores	[7] pain	[8] would	[9] feeble	[10] table
[11] give	[12] wretched	[13] forth	[14] loathsome	[15] carried
[16] riotous	[17] died also	[18] eyes		

Quhen Lazarus he saw with him also
  In his bosome, he said with drerie [1] spreit :
Father Abraham have mercy on my wo,
  Send Lazarus his finger for to weit,[2]
  And cule my toung with cauld water and sweit ;
For I am torment sair into this flame.
Then answerit him our father Abraham,

Remember, son, that thow ressavit hes
  Into thy lyfe thy plesure in all thing.
And, contrariwise, Lazarus had distres,
  Bot now he is in joy and comforting,
  And thow art now in wo and tormenting ;
And als betuix us thair is sa greit ane space
That nane may cum till uther be na cace.[3]

And then he said, O Father, I the pray,
  Unto my fatheris hous thow wald him send
That he my fyve Brether adverteis [4] may,
  Leist thay into this cairfull [5] place discend.
  Bot Abraham said, Let them repent and mend,
And als thay have the Prophetis and Moyses law,
Let them heir them, gif [6] thay the way wald knaw.

Bot he said, Na, my father Abraham kynde,
  Gif ony to the quick yeid [7] from the deid,
Trewly thay suld repent with hart and mynde.
  Bot not the les, Abraham this answer maid,
  Gif thay heir not the Law quhilk suld them leid
Then sall thay nocht in ony wayis beleif,
Thocht ane from deid suld ryse them to releif.

Unto the pure thairfoir be pietifull,
   Quhill ye ar heir schaw them your cheritie,
Till freind and fa be all tyme mercyfull,
   As ye forgive ye sall forgiven be ;
   Mortifie lust and sensualitie,
Conforme yow not to warldly pomp and pryde,
Dreid God, lufe man, refraine lust at all tyde.[1]

7

To us is borne a bairne [2] of blis,
   Our King and Empreour,
Ane gracious Virgin mother is,
   To God hir Saviour.
Had not that blissit bairne bene borne.
We had bene everie ane forlorne
   With Sin and feindis fell.[3]
Christ Jesus, loving be to the
That thow ane man wald borne be,
   To saif us from the hell.

For never was, nor sall be man,
   Nor woman in this lyfe :
Sen Adam first our sin began,
   And Eve his weddit wyfe,
That can be saif throw thair gude deid [4] ;
For poysound all ar Adamis seid,
   And can not sin refraine ;
Quhill God him self sand [5] the remeid,
And gave his only Sone to the deid,
   To freith [6] us from all paine.

---

[1] time   [2] child   [3] cruel
[4] deed   [5] sent   [6] free

We suld lufe God and myrrie be,
  And dryve away despair ;
For Christ is cummin from hevin sa hie,
  Our fall for to repair.
Na toung sic kyndnes can expres :
The form of servand takin hes,
  And Verbum caro factum est [1] ;
Except Sin, lyke unto us all,
To freith us from the Feindis thrall,
  And mend quhair we did mis.

Full weill is them for ever moir,
  That trowis [2] faithfullie,
Be grace to ring [3] with Christ in gloir,
  Throw faith allanerlie [4] :
And weill is them that understude,
The gracious gift of Christis blude,
  Sched sinners for to win :
Was never hard sa kynde ane thing ;
Christ for his fais on Croce did hing,
  To purge us from our sin.

Thus thank we him full hartfully,
  For his greit gentilnes ;
We pray him, for his greit mercy,
  Trew Preichouris till incres ;
Fals Pharesians, and fenyeit lair,[5]
Quhome we have followit lait and air,[6]
  Baith them and us forgive,
God, Father, Sone and Haly Spreit,
Instruct us in thy word sa sweit,
  And efter it to live.

---

[1] " The Word was made flesh "   [2] believes
[3] reign   [4] only
[5] feigned learning   [6] late and early

8

In dulci jubilo,[1] now let us sing with mirth and jo,[2]
Our hartis consolatioun lyis in praesepio [3] ;
And schynis as the Sone, Matris in gremio.[4]
Alpha es et O,[5] Alpha es et O.

O Jesu parvule,[6] I thrist [7] sore efter the :
Confort my hart and mynde, O Puer optime ! [8]
God of all grace sa kynde, et Princeps gloriae,[9]
Trahe me post te ; Trahe me post te.[10]

Ubi sunt gaudia,[11] in ony place, bot thair
Quhair that the angellis sing, Nova Cantica,[12]
Bot and the bellis ring, in Regis curia.[13]
God gif [14] I war thair : God gif I war thair !

[1] In a pleasant joyful cry	[2] joy
[3] in the manger	[4] in the bosom of His Mother
[5] Thou art Alpha and Omega	[6] O tiny Jesus
[7] thirst	[8] Best of children
[9] Prince of glory	[10] Draw me after thee
[11] Where are rejoicings	[12] New songs
[13] In the King's court	[14] give

The Latin original is still in use. A similar version to this was written in German at an earlier date.

9

Till Christ, quhome I am haldin [1] for to lufe,
  I gif my thirlit [2] hart in governance.
How suld I lufe and fra his treuth remufe,
    Full wo wer me, that drerie disseverance,
    Is na remeid, saif only esperance [3] :
For weill, for wo, for boist,[4] or yit for schoir,[5]
Quhair I am set, I sall lufe ever moir.

And sen I must depart on neid, I sall
  Be till him trew, with hart, and that I hecht,[6]
And sen that I becummin am his thrall,
    With body him serve, with mynde and all my micht :
    He is the rute of my remembrance richt,
The verray crop, quhome of I comfort tak :
Quhy suld I not do service for his saik ?

Quhome suld I serve, bot him that did me save ?
  Quhome suld I dout, bot him that dantis [7] deid ?
Quhome suld I lufe, bot him attour the lave ? [8]
    Of all my wo he is the haill remeid :
    How suld I fle, and can not find na feid ? [9]
Quhome suld I lufe, bot him that hes my hart ?
How suld we twin,[10] that na man can depart ? [11]

Thus umbeset I am on everie syde,[12]
  And quhat to do I can not weill devise :
My flesche biddis fle, my spreit biddis me byde :
    Quhen cair cummis, then Comfort on me cryis ;
    Hope sayis get up, then languor on me lyis,
My panis biddis my wofull hart repent,
Bot never mair thairto will I consent.

---

[1] compelled	[2] bound	[3] hope	[4] boasting
[5] threatening	[6] promise	[7] subdues	[8] above the rest
[9] strife	[10] separate	[11] part	[12] beset on every side

Depart him fra, my hart will never consent ;
   It biddis me byde, and I sall never fle ;
For be I takin, slaine, or yit schent,[1]
   For sic ane King it is na schame to die.
   Gif thair be grace into this eird for me,
It is committit from the hevin abufe,
Till Christ quhome I am haldin for to lufe.

10

Richt soirly musing in my mynde,
For pitie soir my hart is pynde,[2]
Quhen I remember on Christ sa kynde,
    that savit me :
Nane culd me saif from Thyle till Ynde,
    bot only He.

He is the way, trothe, lyfe, and licht,
The verray port till hevin full richt,
Quha enteris not be his greit micht
    ane theif is he :
That wald presume be his awin [3] micht
    savit to be.

I grant that I have faultit [4] soir,
To stok and stane gevand his gloir,
And heipand [5] warkis into stoir,
    for my remeid :
War not his mercy is the moir,
    I had bene deid.

---

[1] destroyed   [2] pained   [3] own
     [4] faulted, erred   [5] heaping

Thow lytill bill [1] thy wayis thow wend,
And schaw my mynde fra end to end,
Till them that will repent and mend,
    thow schaw them till :
Beleve in Christ quhome God hes send,
    and wirk his will.

II

Of mercy yit he passis all,
In quhome I traist and ever sall,
For to nane uther will I call,
    To die thairfoir, to die thairfoir.

For thair is nane uther salvatioun
Bot be that Lord that sufferit Passioun ;
Upon our saulis he hes compassioun,
    And deit [2] thairfoir, and deit thairfoir.

That Lord sa far had us in mynde,
He come from hevin and tuke mankynde ;
He haillit [3] the seik, sair, lamit and blinde,
    And deit thairfoir, and deit thairfoir.

To pray to Peter, James, or Johne,
Our Saullis to saif, power have thay none,
For that belangis to Christ allone,
    He deit thairfoir, he deit thairfoir.

I traist to God of suretie,
Be Christis blude savit to be,
In quhilk I hope sa faithfullie,
    To die thairfoir, to die thairfoir.

---

[1] little writing   [2] died   [3] healed

Thair is na deidis,[1] that can save me,
Thocht thay be never sa greit plentie ;
Bot throw Christ, and his greit mercy,
   Quhilk deit thairfoir, quhilk deit thairfoir.

Gif[2] deidis micht save our Saulis from paine,
Then Christis blude was sched in vaine,
As ye may reid in Scripture plaine,
   To die thairfoir, to die thairfoir.

Yit sum hes hope savit to be
For doing deidis of cheritie ;
Faith can not save quhair na deidis be,
   Thay lie thairfoir, thay lie thairfoir.

The thief was saift[3] be faith trewlie,
And not for deidis of cheritie,
As wrytis Luk, twentie and thre,
   To die thairfoir, to die thairfoir.

Fyre without heit can not be,
Faith will have warkis of suretie,
As fast as may convenientlie
   Be done, but[4] moir.

Now Lord, that deit upon ane tre,
And sched thy blude sa plenteouslie
Ressave our Saulis to thy gloir
   We ask no moir, we ask no moir.

[1] deeds   [2] if   [3] saved   [4] without

12

We suld beleve in God abufe,
  And in nane uther thing :
Quha traists in him, he will them lufe,
  And grant them thair asking.

Contrair it is to Goddis command,
  To trow that help may cum,
Of Idoles maid be mennis hand,
  Quhilk ar baith deif and dum.

Quha dois adorne [1] Idolatrie,
  Is contrair the haly writ :
For stock and staine is Mammontrie,[2]
  Quhilk men may carve or quhite.[3]

The Apostillis that wrait the veritie,
  Expresly do conclude,
That Idoles suld detestit be,
  As contrair to Christis blude.

Ye sempill pepill unperfyte,
  Greit ignorance may ye tell,
Of stock and staine hes mair delyte,
  Than into God him sell.

---

[1] adore   [2] idolatry   [3] cut

13

Let us rejoyce and sing,
And praise that michtie King,
   Quhilk send his Sone of a Virgin bricht.
        La.   Lay.   La.

And on him tuke our vyle nature,
Our deidlie woundis to cure,
   Mankynde to hald in richt.
        La.   Lay.   La.

Sanct Luk wrytis in his Gospell,
God send his Angell Gabriell,
   Unto that Virgin but defame,[1]
        La.   Lay.   La.

For to fulfill the Prophesie,
Was spousit [2] with Josaph fre,
   Mary scho had to name.
        La.   Lay.   La.

Thir wordis to her he did reheirs.
Haill Mary ! full of grace,
   The Lord God is with the.
        La.   Lay.   La.

Thow blyssit Virgin mylde,
Thow sall consave ane Chylde
   The pepill redeme sall he :
        La.   Lay.   La.

[1] without reproach   [2] espoused

Quhais power and greit micht,
Sall be in Goddis sicht,
    Quhilk from the Father of micht is send,
        La.   Lay.   La.

Jesus his name ye call,
Quhilk salbe Prince ouir all
    His Kingdome sall have nane end.
        La.   Lay.   La.

Than spak that Virgin fre,
Behald, how sall this be
    Seeing I knaw na man ?
        La.   Lay.   La.

Than said the Angell chaist,
Be the power of the Haly Gaist,
    Quhilk all thing wirk he can.
        La.   Lay.   La.

Elizabeth thy cousing also,
Sex monethis with chylde can go,
    At quhais birth greit joy sall be.
        La.   Lay.   La.

Call him Johne, sayis the Angell bricht,
Quhilk is send be Goddis micht,
    The Lordis way prepair sall he.
        La.   Lay.   La.

*Heir endis the Spirituall Sangis, and beginnis The
Psalmes of David, with other new pleasand
Ballattis. Translatit out of Enchiridion* [1]
Psalmorum, to be sung

14

O Lord, how lang for ever wil thow foryet,
And hyde thy face fra me ? or yit how lang
Sall I reheirs thy counsell in my hart ?
Quhen sall my hart ceis of this sorie sang ?
O Lord, behald, help me, and licht my eine,
That suddand sleip of deid do me na teine.[2]

Or ellis quhen my enemeis seis my fall,
We did prevaill, sone will thay say on me :
And gif thay se me be thame brocht in thrall,
Thay will rejoyce into thair tyrannie.
Bot I in God hes hope, and traist to se
His godly help ; than sall I love the Lord
Quhilk did me save fra thame that had me schord.[3]

---

[1] " Enchiridion " is the term generally borne, according to
Professor Mitchell, by a number of German Lutheran hymn books
issued between 1524 and 1545.

[2] injury   [3] threatened

15

Quha on the Hiest will depend,
   And in his secreit help will traist,
Almichtie God sall him defend,
   And gyde him with his Haly Gaist.
   Thairfoir with mynde rype and degest,[1]
Thow say to God, My trew releve,
   My hope, my God of michtis maist,
Onlie in him I will beleve.

He sall delyver the at neid,
   And save thy lyfe from pestilence ;
His wingis ar thy weirlie weid,[2]
   His pennis [3] ar thy strang defence ;
   And thow sall have experience,
That his trew promeis is thy scheild ;
   His word of grit magnificence
Sall be thy buklar and thy beild.[4]

Na wickit spreit sall the affray,[5]
   Nor the delude into the nicht ;
The fleand dartis [6] be the day,
   To trubill the sall have na micht ;
   Na suddand chance of uncouth slicht.[7]
Sall cummer [8] the, nor mak the red,[9]
   Nor the perturb in mark [10] nor licht,
Bot from all plague thow sall be fred.

And thow sall se at thy left hand,
   Ane thousand have ane suddand fall ;
And als thow sall se ten thousand
   At thy richt hand, quhilk perische sall.

[1] steadfast	[2] warlike dress	[3] pinions	[4] shelter
[5] terrify	[6] flying arrows	[7] cunning	[8] cumber
	[9] afraid	[10] dark	

Yit nocht to the sall cum at all :
Bot thow sall with thine eine behald,
   Sinnaris put fra memoriall,
With plagues grit and monyfald.

O Lord my hope and all my grace,
   Thow save me for thy grit mercy ;
Thy gyrth[1] is set in sicker[2] place,
   For he sall save the michtfullie.
   And na mischance sall cum to the,
Nor maledie sall the molest ;
   Na misfortoun thy hous sall se,
Bot all thingis wirk sall for the best.

His Angellis he sall give ane charge,
   That thay on the sall tak the cure,[3]
In all thy wayis to be ane targe,[4]
   To keip the from misaventure ;
   And with thair handis thay sall the sure,[5]
That thow hurt nocht aganis ane craig[6]
   Thy fute, bot sall preserve the sure
From perrellis, panis, and from plague.

Thow sall strampe on the edderis stang,[7]
   And tred on the cruell cocketrice ;
The lyonnis craig[8] thow sall ouer gang,
   The dreidfull dragoun thow sall chase.
   Sen thow me traistis in all case,
Sayis God, I sall the save from schame,
   And the defend in everie place,
For cause thow knew my godly name.

[1] sanctuary   [2] sure   [3] charge, care   [4] shield   [5] assure
[6] rock   [7] trample on the adder's sting   [8] throat

Quhen thow sall call, I sall the heir,
   And in distres sall be with the.
I sall restoir the haill and feir,[1]
   And als I sall the magnifie :
    With lang lyfe dotit [2] sall thow be,
And at the last I sall the bring
   Quhair thow eternall gloir sall se,
For ever moir with me to ring.

16

Except the Lord with us had stand,
   Say furth, Israell unfenyeitlie,
Had not the Lord bene our warrand,
   Quhen men rais in our contrarie,[3]
They had us all on live devorit,
With ire sa scharpelie thay us schorit,[4]
   Sa kendlit was thair crueltie.

For lyke the welterand wallis brym,[5]
   Thay had ouerquhelmit us with micht ;
Lyke burnis [6] that in spait [7] fast rin,
   Thay had ouerthrawin us with slicht.[8]
The bulrand [9] stremis of thair pryde,
Had pcirsit [10] us throw bak and syde,
   And reft [11] fra us our lyfe full richt.

Bot loving to the Lord, allone,
   That gave us nocht to be thair pray,
To be rent with thair teith anone,
   Bot hes us fred full well thame fray.

---

[1] whole and strong   [2] endowed
[3] opposition   [4] threatened   [5] rolling waves raging
[6] streams   [7] flood   [8] cunning   [9] roaring
     [10] pierced   [11] snatched

Lyke to ane bird taine [1] in ane net,
The quhilk the foullar [2] for her set,
   Sa is our lyfe weill win [3] away.

The net is broken in pecis small,
   And we are savit fra thair schame ;
Our hope was ay and ever sall
   Be in the Lord, and in his Name :
The quhilk hes creat hevin sa hie,
And maid the eird sa mervellouslie,
   And all the ferleis [4] of the same.

17

Quho is at my windo ? quho, quho ?
Go from my windo, go, go !
Quho callis thair, sa lyke ane stranger ?
   Go from my windo, go !

Lord, I am heir, ane wretchit mortall,
That for thy mercy dare cry and call
Unto the, my Lord celestiall.
   Se quho is at thy windo, quho.

How dar thow for mercy cry,
Sa lang in sin as thow dois ly ?
Mercy to have thow art not worthy.
   Go from my windo, go.

My gylt, gude Lord, I will refuse,
And the wickit lyfe that I did use,
Traistand thy mercy sall be myne excuse.
   Se quho is at thy windo, quho.

---

[1] taken   [2] fowler   [3] escaped   [4] wonders

To be excusit, thow wald richt faine,
In spending of thy lyfe in vaine,
Having my Gospell in greit disdaine.
　　Go from my windo, go.

O Lord, I have offendit the,
Excuse thairof thair can nane be :
I have followit tham that sa teichit[1] me.
　　Se quho is at thy windo, quho.

Nay, I call the nocht fra my dure,[2] I wis,
Lyke ane stranger that unknawin is ;
Thow art my brother, and my will it is
　　That in at my dure thow go.

With richt humbill hart, Lord, the I pray,
Thy comfort and grace obteine I may :
Schaw me the path and reddy way
　　In at thy dure for to go.

I am cheif gyde to riche and pure,
Schawand the pathway richt to my dure,
I am thair comfort in everie hour,
　　That in at my dure will go.

Bot thay that walk ane uther way,
As mony did teiche from day to day,
Thay wer indurit,[3] my Gospell did say,
　　And far from my dure sall go.

O gracious Lord, comfort of all wicht,[4]
For thy greit power, and excellent micht,
Sen thow art gyde, and verray licht,
　　In at thy dure lat me go.

---

[1] taught　　　[2] door　　　[3] hardened　　　[4] man

Man, I gave the nocht fre will,
That thow suld my Gospell spill [1];
Thow dois na gude bot ever ill ;
   Thairfoir from my dure that thow go.

That will, allace, hes me begylit,
That will sa sair hes me defylit,
That will thy presence hes me exilit ;
   Yit in at thy dure lat me go.

To blame that will, thow dois not richt,
I gave the ressoun, quhairby thow micht
Have knawin the day by the dark nicht,
   In at my dure for to go.

Lord, I pray the with all my hart,
Of thy greit mercy remufe my smart,[2]
Lat ane drop of thy grace be my part,
   That in at thy dure I may go.

I have spokin in my Scripture,
I will the deid [3] of na creature ;
Quha will ask mercy, sall be sure
   And in at my dure for to go.

O Lord, quhais mercy is but [4] end,
Quhairin ocht [5] to the I did offend,
Grant me space my lyfe to amend,
   That in at thy dure I may go.

Remember thy sin, and als thy smart,
And als for the quhat was my part :
Remember the speir that thirlit [6] my hart,
   And in at my dure thow sall go.

[1] corrupt, mar   [2] pain   [3] death   [4] without
    [5] aught   [6] pierced

And it wer yit till [1] do againe,
Rather or thow suld ly in paine,
I wald suffer mair in certaine,
    That in at my dure thow micht go.

I ask na thing of the thairfoir,
Bot lufe for lufe, to lay in stoir :
Gif me thy hart, I ask no moir,
    And in at my dure thow sall go.

O gracious Lord celestiall,
As thow art Lord and King eternall,
Grant us grace, that we may enter all,
    And in at thy dure for to go.

Quho is at my windo ? quho ?
Go from my windo, go !
Cry na mair thair, lyke ane stranger,
    Bot in at my dure thow go.

18

All my hart, ay this is my sang,
    With doubill mirth and joy amang ;
Sa blyith as byrd my God to sang :
    Christ hes my hart ay. [2]

Quha hes my hart bot hevinnis King ;
    Quhilk causis me for joy to sing,
Quhome that I lufe atouir all thing :
    Christ hes my hart ay.

[1] to   [2] always

He is fair, sober, and bening,[1]
  Sweit, meik, and gentill in all thing,
Maist worthiest to have loving :
    Christ hes my hart ay.

For us that blissit bairne was borne ;
  For us he was baith rent and torne ;
For us he was crownit with thorne ;
    Christ hes my hart ay.

For us he sched his precious blude ;
  For us he was naillit [2] on the rude [3] ;
For us he in mony battell stude ;
    Christ hes my hart ay.

Nixt him, to lufe his Mother fair,
  With steidfast hart, for ever mair ;
Scho bure [4] the byrth, fred us from cair ;
    Christ hes my hart ay.

We pray to God that sittis abufe,
  Fra him let never our hartis remufe,
Nor for na suddand warldly lufe :
    Christ hes my hart ay.

He is the lufe of luifaris all,
  He cummis on him quhen we call ;
For us he drank the bitter gall :
    Christ hes my hart ay.

[1] benign   [2] nailed   [3] cross   [4] bore

C

19

My Lufe murnis for me, for me ;
   My lufe that murnis for me ;
I am not kynde, hes nocht in mynde,
   My Lufe that murnis for me.

Quha is my lufe, bot God abufe,
   Quhilk all this warld hes wrocht ?
The King of blis, my lufe he is,
   Full deir he hes me bocht.

His precious blude he sched on rude,
   That was to mak us fre :
This sall I preve, be Goddis leve,
   That sair my luve murnis for me.

This my lufe comes from abufe,
   And borne was of ane maid ;
For till fulfill his Fatheris will,
   Till fill [1] furth that he said.

Man have in mynde, and thow be kynde,
   Thy lufe that murnis for the,
How he on rude [2] did sched his blude,
   From Sathan to mak the fre.

[1] fulfil   [2] cross

20

Johne, cum kis me now,
Johne, cum kis me now ;
Johne, cum kis me by and by
And mak no moir adow.[1]

The Lord thy God I am,
That Johne dois the call ;
Johne representit man,
Be [2] grace celestiall.

For Johne, Goddis grace it is,
(Quha list till expone the same) [3] :
Och, Johne, thow did amis,
Quhen that thow loste this name.

Hevin and eirth of nocht,
I maid them for thy saik :
For ever moir I thocht
To my lykenes the mak.

In Paradice I plantit the,
And maid the Lord of all
My creatures, not forbidding the
Na thing, bot ane of all.

Thus wald thow not obey,
Nor yit follow to my will :
Bot did cast thyself away,
And thy posteritie spill.[4]

[1] ado   [2] by   [3] cares to expound   [4] destroy

My justice condempnit the
To everlasting paine,
Man culd find na remedie,
To buy man fre againe.

Of pure lufe, and meir mercy,
Myne awin Sone downe I send,
God become man for the,
For thy sin his lyfe did spend.

Thy attonement and peace to mak,
He sched his blude maist halie,
Suffering deith for thy saik,
Quhat culd he do moir for the ?

It plesit Christ, without desart,
For his enemie to die,
Suffering a speir to peirs his hart,
The caus was thy folie.

Beleve this, repent thy sin,
His deith have ever in mynde,
Remissioun of sin lyis only thairin,
To thy Lord be never unkynde.

Quhen he ascendit he left behind
His word to reid and heir,
Quhen Antichrist wald the blind,
That thow suld give him na eir.

Bot quhen Sathan was lowsit [1] out of hell,
And had set man in my place,
All that he did thow thocht it weill,
At him thow socht for grace.

---

[1] loosed

Na thing regarding, how of me
All thing had thair creatioun ;
Nor yit quhat Christ sufferit for the,
To redeme the from dampnatioun.

Bot the abhominatioun of desolatioun,
Thow settis in the haly place,
Be Antichristis fals perswasioun
My Sonnis passioun to deface.

Quhairfoir my justice movit me
My word fra the restraine,
And to thy lust to give up the,
To traist in thingis vaine.

In mannis warkis then did thow traist,
Seiking helth thow wist not quhair,
At thy deith thow did mistraist
And sa fell in despair.

Quhen I did draw ony to me,
My Gospell to profes,
Thow did them slay richt cruellie,
Thinkand to do me service.

Thy service sall rewardit be
With everlasting paine,
And all that hait my word and me,
Except thay do abstene.

Thus, quhen thow was in dangerous case,
Reddy to sink in hell,
Of my mercy and speciall grace,
I send the my Gospell.

My Prophetis call, my preichouris cry,
Johne, cum kis me now,
Johne, cum kis me by and by,
And mak no moir adow.

Ane Spreit I am incorporate,[1]
Na mortall eye can me se,
Yit my word dois intimate,
Johne, how thow must kis me.

Repent thy sin unfenyetlie ;
Beleve my promeis in Christis deith ;
This kis of faith will justifie the,
(As my Scripture plainely saith.)

Mak na delay, cum by and by,
Quhen that I do the call,
Lest deith do stryke the suddanelie,
And sa cum nocht at all.

Gif thow cum nocht quhill thow hes space,
Bot my Gospell dois contempne,[2]
I will tak from the my grace,
And my word will the condempne.

Of all that cum I will none reject,
Na creature greit nor small :
For Christis saik I will them accept,
And give them lyfe eternall.

---

[1] without bodily shape   [2] despise

21

Go, hart, unto the Lamp of licht,
  Go, hart, do service and honour ;
Go, hart, and serve him day and nicht,
  Go, hart, unto thy Saviour.

Go, hart, to thy only remeid,
  Descending from the hevinlie tour,[1]
The to deliver from pyne [2] and deid ;
  Go, hart, unto thy Saviour.

Go, hart, but dissimulatioun,
  To Christ, that tuke our vyle nature,
For the to suffer Passioun ;
  Go, hart, unto thy Saviour.

Go, hart, richt humbill and full meik,
  Go, hart, as leill [3] and trew servitour,[4]
To him that heill [5] is for all seik ;
  Go, hart, unto thy Saviour.

Go, hart, with trew and haill [6] intent,
  To Christ, thy help and haill succour ;
The to redeme he was all rent ;
  Go, hart, unto thy Saviour.

To Christ, that rais from deith to lyve,
  Go, hart, unto my latter hour,
Quhais greit mercy can nane discryve [7] ;
  Go, hart, unto thy Saviour.

[1] tower   [2] pain   [3] loyal   [4] servant
    [5] health   [6] whole   [7] describe

22

Musing greitly in my mynde,
The folie that it is in mankynde,
Quhilk is sa brukill [1] and sa blind,
   And downe sall cum, downe ay, downe ay.

Levand [2] maist pairt in all vice,
Nouther sa gracious, nor sa wyse,
As out of wretchitnes to ryse,
   Bot downe to cum, downe ay, downe ay.

And all this warld to weild [3] thow had,
Thy body perfit and properlie maid,
Yit man, as floure, thow sall faid,
   And downe thow sall cum, downe ay.

Thocht thow war ever eternall,
As man that never suld have ane fall,
Yit doutles die thow sall,
   And downe sall cum, downe ay, downe ay.

Thocht thow war man never sa thrall,[4]
Remember yit that die thow sall ;
Quha hiest clymmis [5] gettis greitest fall,
   And downe sall cum, downe ay, downe ay.

Thocht thow war never of sa greit degre,
In riches nor in dignitie,
Remember, man, that thow mon die,
   And downe sall cum, downe ay, downe ay.

---

[1] frail   [2] living   [3] possess
    [4] enslaved, poor   [5] climbs

Thair is na King, nor Empreour,
Duke, nor Lord of greit valure,
Bot he sall faid as lely floure,
 And downe sall cum, downe ay, downe ay.

Quhair is Adam, and Eve his wyfe,
And Hercules, with his lang stryfe,
And Matussalem,[1] with his lang lyfe ?
 They all ar cum downe ay, downe ay.

23

With huntis up, with huntis up,
 It is now perfite day,
Jesus, our King, is gane in hunting,
 Quha lykis to speid thay may.

Ane cursit fox lay hid in rox
 This lang and mony ane day,
Devoring scheip, quhill he micht creip,
 Nane micht him schaip [2] away.

It did him gude to laip [3] the blude
 Of young and tender lammis ;
Nane culd he mis, for all was his,
 The young anis with thair dammis.

The hunter is Christ, that huntis in haist,
 The hundis ar Peter and Paull,
The Paip is the fox, Rome is the rox,
 That rubbis us on the gall.

---

[1] Methuselah   [2] scare   [3] lap

That cruell beist, he never ceist,
  Be his usurpit power,
Under dispens to get our pence,
  Our saulis to devoir.

Quha culd devyse sic merchandise
  As he had thair to sell,
Onles it war proud Lucifer,
  The greit maister of Hell.

He had to sell the Tantonie bell,[1]
  And pardonis thairin was ;
Remissioun of sinnis in auld scheip skinnis,
  Our saulis to bring from grace.

With bullis of leid,[2] quhyte wax and reid,
  And uther quhylis [3] with grene,
Closit in ane box, this usit the fox,
  Sic peltrie [4] was never sene.

With dispensatiounis and obligatiounis,
  According to his law,
He wald dispens, for money from hence,
  With thame he never saw.

To curs and ban the sempill pure [5] man,
  That had nocht to fle the paine ;
Bot quhen he had payit all to ane myte,
  He mon be absolvit than.

To sum, God wot, he gave tot quot,[6]
  And uther sum pluralitie ;

[1] Tantonie bell : the small jingling bell carried by pardoners—
from the French " tintonner." I can find no grounds for connecting
the word with St Anthony, as previous editors have done.
[2] lead   [3] times   [4] trash   [5] simple poor
[6] " toties quoties " Indulgence : available on as many separate
occasions in one day as the recipient fulfils the conditions stipulated.

Bot first with pence he mon dispens,
  Or ellis it will nocht be.

Kingis to marie, and sum to tarie,[1]
  Sic is his power and micht,
Quha that hes gold, with him will he hold,
  Thocht it be contrair all richt.

O blissit Peter, the fox is ane lier,[2]
  Thow knawis weill it is nocht sa,
Quhill at the last, he salbe downe cast
  His peltrie, pardonis, and all.

24

Baneist [3] is faith now everie quhair,
  And sair forthinkis [4] me :
Baneist is faith now everie quhair
Be the schavin sort,[5] I yow declair.
Allace ! thairfoir my hart is sair,
  And blyith I can nocht be.

Quhair we war wount to go richt glaid,
  Furth of captivitie ;
Quhair we war wount to go richt glaid,
Now have thay us with chargis ouerlaid,
Quhilk bene sa dampnabill, and sa sad,
  That blyith we can nocht be.

---

[1] tarry   [2] liar   [3] banished
[4] repents   [5] shaven kind, the monks

Thay keip the key from us, allace,
  Quhairby enter suld we :
Thay keip the key from us, allace,
And puttis us downe all mercyles ;
We ar ouerthrawin in everie place,
  That blyith we can nocht be.

Ryse up, I pray the now, sweit Lord,
  And from thair crueltie :
Ryse up, I pray the now, sweit Lord,
Defend us according to thy word,
Or we sall perische by fyre and sword,
  That shawis the veritie.

25

Allace, unkyndlie, Christ we have exilit,
And of thair fude his flock we have begylit ;
With vanities we have thame lang deludit,
And in fals beleif hes thame includit :
  And ever this was the blating of our queir,[1]
  Fatheris of haly kirk this xv. hunder yeir.

The water of lyfe we gave thame never to drink,
Bot stinkand pulis [2] of everie rottin synk ;
For haly Scripture alluterlie [3] we have mockit,
And with traditionis of men we have thame yockit [4] ;
  And ever this was the blating of our queir,
  Fatheris of haly kirk this xv. hunder yeir.

---

[1] bleating of our choir   [2] pools   [3] utterly   [4] yoked

Man befoir God, sa lang we have preferrit,
Quhill we se now almaist that all is marrit [1] ;
And God him self is grevit and displesit,
And we thairby ar bot lytill easit ;
    Althocht it be the blating of our queir,
    Fatheris of haly kirk this xv. hunder yeir.

Our blind desyris sen we may nocht fulfill,
Welcum, gude Lord, full sair aganis our will ;
Yit nocht the les we sall do as we may,
And efter this luke for ane better day ;
    And yit salbe the blating of our queir,
    Fatheris of haly kirk this xv. hunder yeir.

We knaw, as did King Saull, our fatell fall ;
Yit, quhill we die, David persew we sall ;
Suppose we suld wrack our self, and tyne [2]
The feild, and all our kin be hangit syne,[3]
    Yit sall it be the blating of our queir,
    Fatheris of haly kirk this xv. hunder yeir.

Lat Moses preiche to Pharao as he lykis,
Yit sall the pepill be tormentit lyke tykis,[4]
And never depart from Egypt : (gif we may)
We salbe cruellest on the hinmest [5] day.
    Quhen we ar drownit, we sall blait on our beir,
    Fatheris of haly kirk this xv. hunder yeir.

O cankerit cariounis, and O ye rottin stakis,
O stangand [6] adderis, and O ye poysound snakis,
Sen ye will nocht change your indurit [7] will,
Knawand your fault, yit will continew still :
    Sing on guk, guk, the blating of your queir,
    Fals fatheris of haly kirk this xv. hunder yeir.

---

[1] marred   [2] lose   [3] after   [4] dogs
    [5] hindmost   [6] stinging   [7] hardened

26

God send everie Preist ane wyfe,
  And everie Nunne ane man,
That thay micht leve that haly lyfe,
  As first the Kirk began.

Sanct Peter, quhome nane can reprufe,
  His lyfe in mariage led :
All gude preistis quhome God did lufe,
  Thair maryit wyfis had.

Greit causis than, I grant, had thay,
  Fra wyfis to refraine :
Bot greiter causis have thay may
  Now wyfis to wed againe.

For than suld nocht sa mony hure
  Be up and downe this land ;
Nor yit sa mony beggeris pure
  In kirk and mercat [1] stand.

And nocht sa mekill [2] bastard seid
  Throw out this cuntrie sawin [3] ;
Nor gude men uncouth fry [4] suld feid,
  And all the suith [5] war knawin.

Sen Christis law, and commoun law,
  And Doctouris will admit,
That Preistis in that yock [6] suld draw ;
  Quha dar say contrair it.

---

[1] market   [2] much   [3] sown
[4] strange brood   [5] truth   [6] yoke

27

Preistis, Christ beleve,
And only traist into his blude,
And nocht into your warkis gude,
As plainely Paull can preve.

Preistis, leirne to preiche,
And put away your ignorance ;
Prais onlie God, his word avance,
And Christis pepill teiche.

Preistis, cut your gowne,
Your nukit bonet [1] put away,
And cut your tippet into tway ;
Go preiche from towne to towne.

Preistis, tak your staffe,
And preiche the Evangell on your feit,
And set on sandellis full meit,
Bot cast your pantounis [2] of.

Preistis, keip na gold,
Silver, nor cunze [3] in your purs,
Nor yit twa coitis with yow turs,[4]
Bot schone [5] to keip yow from cold.

Preistis, thole [6] to preiche,
Sen ye your selfis can preiche na thing ;
Or we your brawling downe sall bring,
And na mair with yow fleiche.[7]

---

[1] square cap	[2] slippers	[3] coins	[4] pack
[5] shoes	[6] allow	[7] wheedle	

Preistis, tak na teind,[1]
Except the word of God ye schaw ;
Thocht ye allege your use and law,
It is nocht as ye weind.[2]

Preistis tak na kyis,[3]
The umest [4] claith ye sall quyte [5] claime
Fra sax pure bairnis [6] with thair dame,
A vengeance on yow cryis.

Preistis, burne no mo,
Of wrang delatioun [7] ye may hyre,
And fals witnes na mair inquire,
And let abjuring go.

Preistis, all and sum
Suld call ane Counsell Generall,
And dres all thingis Spirituall ;
Bot thair thay will nocht cum.

Preistis, reid and wryte,
And your fals Cannoun law lat be,
Quhair Papis contrair Scripturis lie,
And contrair Doctouris dyte.[8]

Preistis, pryde yow nocht
Quhat your Counsellis hes conclude
Contrair the writ and Christin blude,
The quhilk sa deir us bocht.

---

[1] tithe   [2] weened, fancied   [3] cows
[4] " The umest claith " : literally " the uppermost cloth " : a reference to a perquisite then usually expected by the parish priest after a burial.
[5] quit   [6] children   [7] accusation   [8] writing

Preistis, curse no moir,
And now your hartis na mair indure [1] ;
Bot on your flockis tak cure,
Or God sall curse yow soir.

Preistis, leif your pryde,
Your skarlat and your velvote soft,
Your hors and mulis coistlie coft, [2]
And jakmen [3] be your syde.

Preistis, sober be,
And fecht not, nouther boist [4] nor schoir [5] ;
Misreule the realme and court no moir,
And to your kirkis fle.

Preistis, mend your lyfe,
And leif your foule sensualitie,
And vyle stinkand chaistitie,
And ilk [6] ane wed ane wyfe.

Preistis, pray na mair
To Sanct Anthone to save thy sow,
Nor to Sanct Bryde to keip thy cow ;
That grevis God richt sair.

Preistis, worship God,
And put away your imagerie,
Your pardonis and fraternitie,
To hell, the way and rod. [7]

Preistis, sell na Mes,
Bot minister that Sacrament,
As Christ, in the New Testament,
Commandit yow expres.

[1] harden   [2] bought   [3] armed men   [4] vaunt
     [5] threaten   [6] each   [7] road

Preistis, put away
Your paintit fyre of purgatorie,
The ground of your idolatrie ;
It is neir Domisday.

Preistis, change your tone,
And sing into your mother tung
Inglis Psalmes, and ye impugne,
Ye will dyne efter none.

Preistis, preif yow men,
And now defend your libertie ;
For France, and for your dignitie,
Ye brak the peace ye ken.

Preistis, now confes,
How ye sa lang did us begyle,
With mony haly bellie wyle,
To leve in idlenes.

Preistis, I yow exhort,
Your office to do perfite ;
For I say nathing in despite,
Sa God mot me support.

28

Till our Gude-man, till our Gude-man,
Keip faith and lufe till our Gude-man.

For our Gude-man in hevin dois ring
In gloir and blis without ending,
Quhair angellis singis ever Osan [1]
In laude and praise of our Gude-man.

Our Gude-man desyris thre thingis :
Ane hart quhair fra contritioun springis,
Syne lufe him best our saullis that wan,
Quhen we war loist [2] to our Gude-man.

And our Gude-man that ever was kynde,
Requyris of us ane faithfull mynde,
Syne cheritabill be with everie clan,
For lufe only of our Gude-man.

Yit our Gude-man requyris moir,
To give na creature his gloir ;
And gif we do, do quhat we can,
We sall be loist to our Gude-man.

And our Gude-man he promeist sure,
To everie faithfull creature
His greit mercy, that now or than
Will call for grace at our Gude-man.

Adam, that our foirfather was,
He loist us all for his trespas ;
Quhais brukill [3] banis we may sair ban,[4]
That gart [5] us lois our awin Gude-man.

[1] Hosanna   [2] lost   [3] frail   [4] curse   [5] caused

Yit our Gude-man, gracious and gude,
For our salvatioun sched his blude
Upon the croce, quhair thair began
The mercyfulnes of our Gude-man.

This is the blude did us refresche ;
This is the blude that mon us wesche :
The blude that from his hart furth ran,
Maid us fre airis [1] till our Gude-man.

Now let us pray, baith day and hour,
Till Christ our only Mediatour,
Till save us on the day that quhan
We sall be judgeit be our Gude-man.

29

The Paip, that pagane full of pryde,
    He hes us blindit lang ;
For quhair the blind the blind dois gyde,
    Na wonder baith ga wrang :
Lyke prince and king he led the ring
    Of all iniquitie :
Hay trix, tryme go trix,
    Under the grene wod-tre.

Bot his abominatioun
    The Lord hes brocht to licht ;
His Popische pryde, and thrinfalde [2] crowne,
    Almaist hes loist thair micht ;
His plak [3] pardonis ar bot lardonis [4]
    Of new found vanitie :
Hay trix, tryme go trix, etc.

[1] heirs   [2] triple
[3] plack, a small coin   [4] lumps

His Cardinallis hes caus to murne,
  His Bischoppis borne aback :
His Abbottis gat ane uncouth [1] turne,
  Quhen schavelingis went to sack ;
With burges wyfis thay led thair lyfis,
  And fure [2] better nor we :
Hay trix, tryme go trix, etc.

His Carmelites and Jacobinis,[3]
  His Dominiks had greit ado ;
His Cordeleiris,[4] and Augustinis,
  Sanct Frances ordour to ;
Thay sillie Freiris, mony yeiris,
  With babling blerit [5] our ee :
Hay trix, tryme go trix, etc.

The Sisteris gray,[6] befoir this day,
  Did crune within thair cloister ;
Thay feit [7] ane freir thair keyis to beir,
  The Feind ressave the foster [8] ;
Syne in the mirk,[9] sa weill culd wirk,
  And kittill [10] thame wantounlie :
Hay trix, tryme go trix, etc.

The blind Bischop he culd nocht preiche,
  For playing with the lassis ;
The syllie Freir behuffit to fleiche,[11]
  For almous that he assis [12] ;
The Curat, his creid he culd nocht reid,
  Schame fall the cumpanie :
Hay trix, tryme go trix, etc.

[1] queer   [2] fared
[3] Dominicans : so-called from the Priory of S. Jacques in **Paris**.
[4] Franciscans   [5] dulled   [6] Probably Franciscan nuns
[7] paid   [8] offspring   [9] dark
[10] tickle   [11] behoved to flatter   [12] asks

The Bischop wald nocht wed ane wyfe,
    The Abbote not persew ane,
Thinkand it was ane lustie lyfe,
    Ilk day to have ane new ane,
In everie place, ane uncouth [1] face,
    His lust to satisfie :
Hay trix, tryme go trix, etc.

The Persoun wald nocht have ane hure,
    Bot twa, and thay war bony [2] :
The Vicar (thocht he was pure),[3]
    Behuiffit to have als mony ;
The pareis [4] Preist, that brutall beist,
    He polit thame privelie :
Hay trix, tryme go trix, etc.

Of Scotland Well, the Freiris of Faill,[5]
    The lymmerie [6] lang hes lestit ;
The Monkis of Melros maid gude kaill [7]
    On Frydayis quhen thay fastit ;
The syllis Nunnis caist up thair bunnis,[8]
    And heisit [9] thair hippis on hie :
Hay trix, tryme go trix, etc.

Of lait I saw thir lymmaris [10] stand,
    Lyke mad men at mischeif,
Thinking to get the upper hand,
    Thay luke efter releif :
Bot all in vaine, go tell thame plaine,
    That day will never be :
Hay trix, tryme go trix, etc.

---

[1] strange   [2] lovely   [3] poor   [4] parish
[5] Priories in Kinross and Ayrshire   [6] villainy   [7] broth
[8] bottoms   [9] heaved   [10] these rascals

O Jesus ! gif thay thocht greit glie,
  To se Goddis word downe smorit,[1]
The Congregatioun [2] maid to flie,
  Hypocrisie restorit ;
With Messis sung, and bellis rung,
  To thair Idolatrie ;
Marie, God thank yow, we sall gar brank [3] yow
  Befoir that tyme trewlie.

30

All my Lufe, leif me not,
  Leif me not, leif me not ;
All my Lufe, leif me not,
  Thus myne alone :
With ane burding [4] on my bak,
I may not beir it I am sa waik ;
Lufe, this burding from me tak,
  Or ellis I am gone.

With sinnis I am ladin soir,
  Leif me not, leif me not ;
With sinnis I am ladin soir,
  Leif me not alone.
I pray the, Lord, thairfoir
Keip not my sinnis in stoir,
Lowse [5] me or I be forloir,
  And heir my mone.

---

[1] smothered
[2] Presumably a reference to the League of Protestant nobles :
" The Lords of the Congregation."
[3] bridle, curb   [4] burden   [5] loose

With thy handis thow hes me wrocht,
  Leif me not, leif me not ;
With thy handis thow hes me wrocht,
  Leif me not alone.
I was sauld, and thow me bocht,
With thy blude thow hes me coft,[1]
Now am I hidder socht
  To the, Lord, alone.

I cry, and I call to the,
  To leif me not, to leif me not ;
I cry, and I call to the,
  To leif me not alone.
All thay that ladin be,
Thow biddis thame cum to the ;
Than sall thay savit be,
  Throw thy mercy alone.

Thow saves all the penitent,
  And leifis thame not, and leifis thame not ;
Thow saves all the penitent,
  And leifis thame not alone.
All that will thair sinnis repent
Nane of them salbe schent [2] ;
Suppose thy bow be reddy bent,
  Of thame thow killis none.

Faith, Hope, and Cheritie,
  Leif me not, leif me not ;
Faith, Hope, and Cheritie,
  Leif me not alone.
I pray the, Lord, grant me,
Thir [3] godly giftis thre ;
Than sall I savit be,
  Dout have I none.

---

[1] bought   [2] destroyed   [3] these

To the Father be all gloir,
　　That leifis us not, that leifis us not ;
To the Father be all gloir,
　　That leifis us not alone.
Sone and Haly Gaist, ever moir,
As it was of befoir ;
Throw Christ our Saviour,
　　We are saif everie one.

31

O Man, ryse up, and be not swier,[1]
Prepair aganis this gude New Yeir.
　　My New Yeir gift thow hes in stoir,
Sen I am he that coft [2] the deir :
　　Gif [3] me thy hart, I ask no moir.

Gif me thy hart, for I suld have it ;
It is my richt, thairfoir I craif it :
　　To win the samin, I sufferit soir,
And now am reddy to ressave it :
　　Gif me thy hart, I ask no moir.

I am the Lord maid the of nocht,
Lyke my awin image hes the wrocht ;
　　The to all frelage [4] I did restoir :
Sen my hart blude thy hart hes bocht,
　　Gif me thy hart, I ask no moir.

I come in eirth, and thair did dwell,
I send na message bot my sell,
　　The to relief of deidly soir :
Sen I have fred the from the hell,
　　Gif me thy hart, I ask no moir.

---

[1] loath　　　[2] bought　　　[3] give　　　[4] freedom

I have the fred from all thirlage,[1]
And hes preparit thyne heritage,
  Quhair deith sall never the devoir :
And now am cummin to craif my wage ;
  Gif me thy hart, I ask no moir.

Be war, I am ane Jelous God,
I am na image, stock nor wod [2] ;
  Thairfoir give nane of thay my gloir,
Sen I to hevin mon be the rod [3] :
  Gif me thy hart, I ask no moir.

Let be thy sculptill honouris vaine,
Quhilkis ar confoundit and prophaine.
  And swa [4] ar all dois them adoir,
As testifyis David in Scripture plaine :
  Gif me thy hart, I ask no moir.

Sen this last yeir thow hes offendit,
Contrair my law thy lyfe hes spendit,
  My mercy is reddy yit, as of befoir :
In this New Yeir all may be amendit :
  Gif me thy hart, I ask no moir.

---

[1] bondage   [2] wood   [3] road   [4] so

32

O man, behald this warldis vaniteis,
   The joy of it I wait [1] is fantasie ;
Thairfoir be war, my counsell now it is :
   Be glaid in God, for doutles thow mon die.

Think thow art cum, and wait not quhen to pas ;
   Think thow mon change, and wait not quhair to be :
Think quhy thow come, and quhat thy erand was :
   Be weill avisit,[2] for doutles thow mon die.

Avise the weill, quhill thow hes tyme and space,
   Exempill tak daylie, as thow may se ;
Quhen deith cummis thair is na uther grace,
   Bot yeild the than, for doutles thow mon die.

Yeild the to God, with humbill hart contrite,
   In cheritie lufe, as thow wald lufit be ;
Gif thow wald leif without this warldis despite,
   Remember on this, for doutles thow mon die.

Remember upon thy God Omnipotent,
   That is and was, and ever moir salbe ;
And for thy sin he saikleslie [3] was schent [4] ;
   Be kynde againe, for doutles thow mon die.

Be kynde againe for hevin celestiall,
   Quhair gloir and joy without end sall be ;
Be kynde, and dreid the cruell paine of hell ;
   Cheis [5] the the ane, for doutles thow mon die.

[1] know   [2] advised   [3] without guilt
    [4] destroyed   [5] choose

INDEX

P : based on a popular secular ballad.

L : on a Lutheran source.

M : on a mediæval hymn.